The
Small Business
Trap

Why Most Entrepreneurs Work Too Hard,
Earn Too Little, and
Can't Grow Their Business

Majeed Mogharreban

The **Small Business** Trap

ISBN-13: 978-0-9988546-0-1
ISBN-10: 0-9988546-0-3

Published by: Celebrity Expert Author
http://celebrityexpertauthor.com

Canadian Address:
1108 - 1155 The High Street,
Coquitlam, BC, Canada
V3B.7W4
Phone: (604) 941-3041
Fax: (604) 944-7993

US Address:
1300 Boblett Street
Unit A-218
Blaine, WA 98230
Phone: (866) 492-6623
Fax: (250) 493-6603

Claim your free gifts at **www.smallbiztrap.com**
and you'll receive…

- Selling With Heart Online Course ($1997 value)

- Special Report: Grant-Getting Secrets To Win Free Government Money ($97 value)

- Free 1-on-1 Freedom Formula Strategy Session with Majeed ($997 value)

TOTAL VALUE $3091

I am honoured that you have taken the time to pick up this book, and I consider you a friend. Please reach out by email at majeed@majeedm.com or phone or text at 1-613-292-1159. I would be happy to offer you a complimentary 9-minute one-on-one strategy session to see if I can support you. Register at www.majeedm.com/strategy.

Here's to your success!
- Majeed

Advance Praise

Majeed's open, powerful message will help you move through obstacles and create a life and business that is a true fit for you. Even as a doctor of psychology, I can see how limiting beliefs and lack of action are obstacles. This book is the answer to overcoming obstacles and creating a life and successful business...for anyone!

- Dr. Denise Morette,
Clinical Psychologist

As a business owner, or even someone who dreams of starting one, this book is a must read! Gaining clarity on where you are wanting to go in life and in business is key, and this book helps you do it! I was able to gain clarity in the direction I wanted to go, get tools for how to get there, change some limiting beliefs, and get the courage to take action on my next step!! It really gave me the motivation I needed to start asking myself the right questions!

- Kim Lavigne,
Owner A Major Media

I read the "Definition" of the Fearless Leader and it's like you crawled into my head!! This is EXACTLY what I need right now in my life and my business!

- Dana Fortier, Owner,
Create Some Buzz

Reading Majeed's book is like being coached by him. Each page contains insightful and inspiring information guaranteed to help any entrepreneur at all stages of business.

- Nicola Wolters,
Strategic Marketing Consultant

After wrapping up a 30yr successful career in the non-profit charity sector I have struggled with "what's next". Your book resonated so strongly with me and the timing couldn't be better. Taking my passion to make a difference; adding real purpose and leaving my mark. Clarity, Creativity only happens with Courage. Your book has given me the missing "C". Here's to a new day!

- Lynn Noel,
National Sales Manager at LTD Radio

Love the "C"s: Clarity - Know what you want. Creativity - have fun! Commitment - decide you will create results. Courage - push your personal boundaries - get uncomfortable. Written from a place of compassion in a way that is easy to bite off, gnaw on, and digest - knowledge is nourishment! Looking forward to applying Majeed's wisdom!

- Dawn Collings,
Business Development at Light Switch Creative Inc

Majeed applies the K.I.S.S. principle beautifully – Keep it Sweetly Simple. There's power in the simplicity Majeed shares with his readers in how Clarity, Creativity, Commitment, and Courage to help them drive their future forward to great success, joy, and satisfaction. Having this book in "your back pocket" is like having Majeed in "your back pocket" – instant coaching!

- Kit Cassingham,
Business Coach

Having been self-employed for 20+ years and just recently stepped it up into business owner status, I found great value in Majeed's Badass Businesswoman Book. Not only did it resonate with me in so many areas, it helped me identify the key areas that required my attention. He writes like he talks: clear, concise and in a way that makes it easy for you to "get it". He provides a different perspective in many areas, jumping to a higher level in creativity - removing "the box". To achieve "Fearless Leader" status it is clear you must have all 4 C's - Clarity is key in understanding your definition of success. This is one book I'll be adding to the 'must reads' for the entrepreneurs I work with and mentor.

- Liz M Raymond,
Professional Business Organizer

Majeed's Fearless Leader definition is incredible! Energetic, insightful and empowering. Majeed writes as if he's talking to me over a cup of coffee in simple easy to digest terms. Clarity, Creativity, Commitment, and Courage. Majeed lays it all on the line in easy-to-follow steps with real-life examples that are relatable to the general population. Using genuine, and sometimes hard, questions and exercises, allows me, the reader, to work through the fog standing in the way of my own Clarity, Creativity, Commitment, and Courage. A highly recommended read.

- Penny Mayo,
Parenting Coach

An easy read and filled with crucial guidance for all entrepreneurs. I didn't realize how one's awareness of their personal past could make such a difference to one's success in business. Definitely a book I'll refer back to more than once!

- Trish Rossiter,
Glass Artisan

This books provides the guidance I have been looking for. Years of overwhelm, the never ending to do list, well meaning opinions of those invested in our success replaced by easier steps that make it possible to align personal priorities with commitment to our passion and purpose to create our own successful model.

- Catherine Corey,
Owner, Spirit Walk Counseling Services

This book is amazing! You will be a FEARLESS LEADER by applying the very clear steps that Majeed has outlined in this amazing book. This book will forever be something I will refer back to in order to keep my goals in check.

- Sylvia Corzato,
Owner, Success In Steps

This book is a delightful read! I couldn't wait to turn the page to see what awesome strategy would pop up next! The anticipation of more juicy content was tempered by the deeply thought provoking questions. My focus for my business has been motivationally impacted by this book. Thank You Majeed!

- Corey Stiles, Owner,
Chyme Studio

This book is like a conversation with Majeed. Reading the personal experiences and realizations of Majeed and his clients was so familiar. It made me realize just how similar our fears are. Every single chapter gives you immediate actionable steps. The true stories motivate you to take the leap and try because what on earth do you have to lose? I've already recommended this book to so many entrepreneurs and business owners because it will move the needle for you!

- Shima Shahidy,
Chiropractor

Master the ways of the Fearless Leader. Learn to master 4 principles that will fine tune your success. Majeed shows you how to take your business by the horns while empowering you with the tools to tame any challenge and rise above. I had such a fun time reading through this book. It's easy to take action and feels like a dialogue between you and Majeed. That's what makes him a great coach. He's easy to talk to and knows how to take you to the next level. Majeed's warm heart and coaching is a real privilege.

- Mary Jennifer Brauner,
Creative Client Attraction Strategist

The most powerful aspect of the book is its rawness! The book represents all the questions I had in my mind that I was too afraid to seek answers for. It's presented in a bite size and hands on format that invites you to look at your core before getting started, recognizing the need to align your behaviours to your inner core as a foundation for success.

-Sarah Bartal,
Business Consultant and Certified Public Accountant

I love how easy it was to read, the wonderful examples you used and the challenges you pose to your reader. An excellent tool for anyone to build their confidence and business. This will help those diamonds in the rough start to shine!

- Julie Schneider,
Black Hawk College

Words and stories of motivation helping you discover the power within. Stories of outstanding entrepreneurs capture and hold your attention throughout the piece, leaving the reader in awe of their brilliance and perseverance. Through this, Majeed brings forth a heartwarming call to action for all entrepreneurs to realize their potential in shattering the norms in business and life. This is a piece all should read, and a tool all should use both to discover their own potential and to help others discover their own in all aspects of their entrepreneurial life.

- Sam Turgeon-Brabazon,
Owner, Sam's Sprouts

*To my courageous, brave clients, past, present, and future,
for putting yourself out there and showing the world what
a Fearless Leader looks like.*

Contents

Fearless Leader Definition 17

Introduction 19

Chapter 1 – Help! I'm Trapped by My Business 27

Chapter 2 – The #1 Reason Why Small Business
Owners Stay Trapped 37

Chapter 3 – Turn Your Most Overlooked Resource
into Massive Profits 47

Chapter 4 – Commit and Grow Rich 61

Chapter 5 – The Fearless Leader Habit That Turns
Problems into Profit 77

Chapter 6 – The Biggest Mistakes That Will Keep You
Trapped 95

Chapter 7 – Next Steps for the Fearless Leader 101

Acknowledgements 105

About the Author 107

Thank You 109

Fearless Leader Definition

1. You define success on your terms.

2. You sell with confidence and close the deal when it really counts.

3. You are an example of positive attitude and you attract positivity.

4. You take care of your body, mind, and business, and thus set the standard for how other people treat you and your team.

5. You are creative and resourceful and see opportunities where others see barriers.

6. You have a vision to transform the world starting with your local community.

7. You have a very low tolerance for bullshit.

As a Fearless Leader you have **Clarity** of what success looks like, **Creativity** to find smarter ways to succeed faster, **Commitment** to make it happen no matter what, and **Courage** to take massive action despite fear and uncertainty.

Introduction

If you're like most entrepreneurs, you started your business because you had a dream. You have a gift that you wanted to bring to the world. You wanted to "be your own boss." You wanted to have freedom and fun and make a difference on your own terms.

How's that working out for you?

If it's not going as well as you had hoped, don't worry, it's perfectly normal. Two out of three businesses fail within the first two years and 50 percent of businesses fail within the first year. If you've made it this far, you have a lot to be proud of. You knew it wouldn't be easy, but you probably didn't think it would be this hard either. Did you?

If you're like most business owners, you feel like you work too hard, don't make as much money as you thought you would, and there are days when you feel like giving up, shutting down your business, and brushing up your resume so you can go look for a job. And that thought makes you sick to your stomach. Am I right?

Your friends seem to think you're a success. You seem happy, you seem successful, and according to your social media posts, your life looks amazing. But at the end of a long work day you drive home feeling tired, lost, and, occasionally, desperate. You feel like you don't take enough time for yourself. You feel like your staff needs you for every little decision, and they can't solve problems on their own. You know there's more to life. You know you were meant for more, but you feel like you just don't have the energy to do anything about it.

Welcome to The Small Business Trap.

This is where 98 percent of small business owners live and they never learn how to escape.

You may find yourself rationalizing that …

"It's just a tough market right now."

"My industry is really competitive."

"Once the right person is hired, everything will be better."

"Once the new software is installed, all our problems will be solved."

The truth is, there are months when your employees are making more money than you are and you wonder to yourself if you'll be able to make payroll next week. It's time to ask yourself a very important question:

How long are you going to put up with this?

Are you going to call it quits and join the statistical majority who tried and failed? Or are you going to be among the 2 percent who make it out of The Small Business Trap?

I love being an entrepreneur. I can't work for anybody else. But I have found myself in The Small Business Trap many times before. My adventurous, freedom-seeking side wants to break free from the chains created by my business. More clients, more work, more responsibility, means less freedom. Or so I thought.

But there is a better way.

I was fortunate to discover The Small Business Trap early on in my path as an entrepreneur.

It all started when I met my wife, Elaine, traveling in Zanzibar, Tanzania, Africa. I was in my fifth cycle of save money, travel, go broke, start over.

Let me explain …

I was born in California to an immigrant father from Iran and a Polish/German mother from Chicago. Dad was a computer programmer and Mom was a schoolteacher. I didn't know a single entrepreneur growing up. As a kid, I only knew to apply for minimum wage jobs, but I found that even as a kid I could run a business and make more money faster than getting a job.

At the age of 16, I started my first business—a snow cone stand that I bought for $12,000 and sold three years later for $24,000. I travelled to South America with the money I got from the sale of the business. After running out of money while traveling, I came back home and start another business, sold it, and travelled again until I was broke. I did this cycle for five businesses, 24 countries, before I was 21 years old. At the end of each cycle, I was broke with no business. But when I had a business, I felt trapped. So the cycle was, start business (trapped), sell business (escape), spend money living life on my terms (broke) … and repeat.

Each time I started a new business, I was back in The Small Business Trap, trapped by my business and unable to travel because I couldn't leave the business.

Could there possibly be a better way? Could I have a business and live life on my terms? The answer is "Yes!" And I have found a way to do it. That's what you will learn in this book.

Today, I run a training and coaching company out of my home office in Gatineau, Quebec, Canada. I spend as much time as I can with my two young children, Ruby and Charlie, and travel with my family whenever possible, taking a two-month work-ation (work/vacation—work half-time from abroad) each year. I get to do the work that I am uniquely talented to do, that I am passionate about, and I work with clients that inspire me. This life and business are not by accident. This is by design.

It wasn't easy to figure this out. Here's how I made it work ...

At the age of 23, I met my amazing Canadian wife on a spice tour in Zanzibar, Tanzania, Africa. I moved to Canada to be with her and started to craft the life and business that we wanted to create. In the beginning, I prioritized opportunities where I could travel for work, because I love to travel; it's even better when the client pays for it.

After having kids, I had to create a whole new way of working. One-hundred-hour workweeks and traveling two to three weeks out of the month wouldn't work anymore. Together with my wife, we designed a lifestyle that we both love while still doing meaningful, profitable work with clients we love.

Breaking Free from The Small Business Trap

To create this business and lifestyle, I used what I now call, **The Freedom Formula**, which you will learn in this book so you can apply it to your business and life.

There are four steps in The Freedom Formula:

1. **Clarity**—know exactly what you want.

2. **Creativity**—find easy and fun ways to get what you want.

3. **Commitment**—decide that you will run your business and life on your terms.

4. **Courage**—take action despite fear and uncertainty.

When you follow The Freedom Formula, you know what you want, you are not afraid to go after it, and you become what I call a Fearless Leader.

Designing the Ideal Business and Ultimate Lifestyle

My accountant and client, Maggie, has crafted and lives her ultimate lifestyle. She works the hours she wants, on the days of the week she wants. She works and meets with clients in a beautiful downtown home office. She also lives at her lake house and invites her favourite clients (like me!) to stay out at that lake house, go out for rides on her boat, and enjoy a deep client/friend relationship. I saw the unconventional lifestyle that she unapologetically created, and I wanted to create something like that for my business.

So, within two years, I bought a duplex. I live in one unit and host clients in the other unit, just like Maggie. I have deep relationships with clients I call friends; I set my own hours and have fun in the process.

That's what I wanted to create. What about you? What is your ideal business? Your ideal office? Ideal client?

Close your eyes and take a moment to imagine your ideal business and ultimate lifestyle.

Here's another example of combining business and pleasure. I love to spend time at the spa and take my clients there, so I decided to host a mastermind retreat called Mastermind Spa at one of my favourite places in the world, Le Nordik Spa, the largest spa in North America and the place where I proposed to my wife.

A mastermind is a group that comes together for the purpose of growing and supporting each other. I carefully curate the group for positive, success-minded individuals that I know will give as much as they receive. This is a time for high-level entrepreneurs to design their ultimate lifestyle, design their business to support that lifestyle, and create the impact and income they desire. If you're interested in creating a business that provides the income, impact, and lifestyle you desire, have a look at www.mastermindspa.com. It's an invitation-only event, so if you're interested send me an email at majeed@majeedm.com.

I love to travel, so for my highest-level clients I provide a year-long mentorship program called Business Mastery and we host international business retreats called Business From The Beach where we create and execute marketing and sales plans during the day, with mini beach breaks, and enjoy local island culture at night.

This is my way of designing the lifestyle I want while serving my clients at the deepest possible level. My lifestyle and business may not be what lights you up. That's not the point. The point is to give you a process to get clear on your ideal life and business and also to give you the tools to start making it happen today.

Today, it is my privilege to work with service business owners who are committed to living a great life while making a huge impact. Best of all, they are running their business in a way that fits their style, strengths, and passions, so it's fun and easy. My process is to first get them super clear on what they really want in their business and life using The Freedom Formula, make as simple a plan as possible, and then execute to get there faster than they ever thought possible. That's exactly what we'll do here in this book.

After taking clients through The Freedom Formula, I have seen some incredible personal and professional results, such as taking more time off while increasing profits, having better relationships with clients and friends, losing weight, or all of the above. This process is nothing short of life changing and I'm really excited for you!

Staff Training Sets You Free

If you own a business with employees, you'll be stuck in The Small Business Trap until you find a way to train your staff to run your business for you without you needing to be there. Large, successful companies budget time and money to train staff to be able to run the organization. Entrepreneurs in The Small Business Trap typically don't have the time or money to invest to properly train staff to run the business without them.

This one investment can set you free, but most businesses don't have a training budget. That's exactly where I was as a small business owner. I needed to learn what big successful companies knew but I didn't have the funds to do it. So I did what I always do. I hacked my way in.

I got hired as an instructor at Learning Tree International, a company that handles the staff training for major Fortune 500 companies and governments around the world. Most of the other consultants there had grey hair and a long list of credentials. At 25 I had neither they grey hair nor the credentials, but what I did have was a background in theater performance, professional speaking, and comedy which made me one of the most entertaining instructors, despite my lack of experience.

Over the seven years that I have been doing work with

Learning Tree International, I have delivered leadership training for large companies and organizations like CitiGroup,
The United Nations, and national and local governments.
I am the #1 highest rated trainer in the world out of 721
trainers at Learning Tree International. On top of all that,
I achieved my goal of figuring out what the big guys knew.
And now I can share world-class training with small business
clients who don't have the budgets for top-tier training pro-
grams.

Who Likes Free Money for Staff Training?

In Canada, and likely wherever you are, there are grants
to pay for staff training. I love helping business owners find
free money to help them escape The Small Business Trap. If
you would like me to show you how to get free government
grants to train your staff, email me at majeed@majeedm.com.

Chapter 1

Help!
I'm Trapped by My Business

Tell me if this sounds familiar. You've been working so hard for so long, and you feel like your business will fall apart without you. You don't feel like you can take a vacation, and some months you don't know if you can even make payroll. You think that if you could only find good people who could sell for you so that you could focus on the fun stuff, and then life would be grand. If this is you, you're not alone. Most people who own their own businesses feel trapped sometimes and wonder if the hustling can ever stop. After all, most of us grew up believing that success requires hard work, and business is supposed to be hard. What if there was a way to make work easy and fun while enjoying even higher levels of success? Well, let me tell you that it is possible.

You probably wish you could just hire someone to sell for you, so that you can focus on doing the fun, creative work and not have to deal with the discomfort of selling. It would make a huge difference. If you could just hire better people who make decisions for themselves and don't need to be constantly managed, you would finally get some freedom from your business.

You may feel bored with some of your current clients, doing work that doesn't light you up, but it pays the bills. What if there was a way to attract your favourite type of clients and repel everyone else? What if you knew exactly who you wanted to work with and you knew how to find those people who really value you for your authentic approach to solving their problem?

You are about to discover that true freedom is within your reach right now, because this book will show you that freedom has less to do with money and more to do with Clarity, Creativity, Commitment, and Courage.

Meet Cathy

I met Cathy after giving a talk on personal branding. She came up to me and told me that she liked my way of thinking about business and getting paid to do what you love. She always wanted to do work that was more interesting with higher profit margins, but she never knew how. She thought personal branding was the answer, but liked my approach to sales. She asked if she could hire me to help grow her business, and I told her we should start with a strategy session to see what her biggest challenges were. Within 15 minutes we had uncovered the core of the issue. The truth was, she was bored with her business, and she didn't have enough time, or at least she believed she didn't, to do anything else.

Sound familiar? How can you grow your business or change your business when you're already working a hundred hours a week? I showed her how we could double her sales without working harder or increasing costs, and she ended up hiring me to coach her and her team.

The "Hard Worker" Block

When I started working with Cathy it was clear that she is an extremely caring mother and is like a mother to her employees. She is a super hard worker. Her dad is a hard worker and appreciates and respects other people who work hard. Guess what? We all want the approval of our parents. So Cathy became a hard worker to get her father's approval, on a subconscious level. If she were to take time for herself, relax, and not work as hard, it wouldn't feel right to her. She would feel lazy. And probably, on a subconscious level, she would feel that her father wouldn't respect her as much. Combine that with the loving, caring energy, she has to take care of her team before she takes care of herself.

When we asked her team of 12 people to take the Strengths Finder 2.0 test, they all had similar characteristics: Hard working, caring, concerned with other's well being, team players … it all started to make sense. Often the business owner sets the tone for the culture. The team was stressed and overworked in the pursuit of putting other people's needs first, including clients and coworkers.

An overworked team does not have the creative energy to make quantum leap improvements. So we put together a wellness plan to help improve diet, exercise, and general self-care. We could immediately see a shift in culture. Jenn, the office manager, quit smoking. Healthy lunches were brought to the office. People were taking regular breaks where before they would "push through" and burn out. Change the culture; change the results.

We had to address the underlying beliefs about hard work and putting others' needs first. After two intensive coaching sessions, Cathy went home and had a self-care revolution. She bought herself an exercise rebounder (my preferred method for energizing and getting movement in the morning). She started having a green smoothie every morning, something that I have implemented in my morning routine that has given me a boost of energy and nutrition every day. She started taking care of herself first, and because of that her business prospered. She was more present, vibrant, focused, and energized. That allowed her to make better decisions, close more deals, and be a better example for her staff.

Within a few short weeks of making these shifts, she stopped taking small jobs, had the confidence to raise her prices, and started landing one 6-figure contract after the other. Cathy started to see her company as a world-class leader in her industry. She believed for the first time that she deserved high fees, and her clients deserved her best work. She decided to no longer be the cheapest choice and to say no to clients that only wanted the lowest price. She decided she would only work with clients that wanted her for her unique gifts and were willing to pay top dollar.

The transformation has been extraordinary. She chooses to only work with her favourite clients, and only do the work that interests her. Other members of her team take on the parts of the business that are not in her area of genius. She has empowered her team to make decisions and to settle disputes and to handle problems on their own. She's removed herself from the day-to-day micromanagement of operating the business so that she can focus her creativity and energy on the work that is most meaningful and exciting for her. For the first time in a long time she loves her business again.

So what really happened? Her self-image and her self-worth went way up. She released the belief she had that her father would only respect her if she worked hard. She came to realize that she will always love her father and that her father will always love her, even if she takes care of herself and works fewer hours.

She made a few difficult decisions. She let go of a team member that she cared dearly about. She knew he wasn't a fit to remain a part of her team, and she was in tears with him when she let him go, because she cared so much about him. They had known it for some time, but she finally had the Courage to take action. She decided to be authentic and vulnerable with her team at a level she had never done before. She started to share her deepest desires for her business, and her team supported her at a deeper level than ever before. She was afraid that her team would reject her vision, but the result was the exact opposite. The team got on board and rallied behind her vision and wanted her to succeed.

I had the honour to facilitate a retreat for Cathy's team to create a deep team connection and to embrace Cathy's vision for the company. We went through a process of recognizing how each person on the team has their own journey and their own ideal life and ideal job and how the company can be their vehicle for their own personal development and fulfillment. Each team member awoke to the fact that their role was more than "just a job." They were part of a family, part of a bigger idea to create excellence in their craft and fully express their talents. They transformed from workers to artists. They went from having personal growth be outside of the office to now making their job their vehicle for self-growth, self-actualization, and personal development.

It's my belief that the best companies in the world create a space for their employees to realize their full potential and creative expression. The best companies in the world are feeding the souls of their employees. It's more than a job …

it's a calling. It is spiritually fulfilling. It is facilitating better health, better relationships.

Cathy hired me to help her with sales. But it wasn't sales training that allowed the sales to grow. It was actually working on the hearts and souls of her team and herself. Everything began to shift once she chose to transform herself into becoming her highest self by raising her standards, by deciding that excellence is a choice, and by demanding the best from herself, from her team, and from her clients, and she started to take care of her body and her soul. In our time together and during her team retreat, we focused on mental and spiritual health. We focused on making the job more than a job by discovering passion and strength and the highest value activities. The result was that work became more fun, easy, and way more profitable.

Cathy is now a Fearless Leader. She wanted to grow her business without feeling trapped by her business, and by taking care of herself and her team, raising her standards, and deciding to only work with her best clients, she was able to make this a reality.

Maybe you don't have a team working for you. Many of my clients don't. But you do have people you work with closely, so I'll refer to them as your "team". These are people you hire for web work, photography, video, rental space, catering, etc. You influence how they treat you by how you treat yourself. Treat yourself like a Fearless Leader, and watch how they start to treat you better!

How To Make Business Easy and Fun

I grew up hearing over and over that business is hard, business is risky, work is not supposed to be fun, and you take vacations to "get away from it all." And I believed it. And for years and years I made it hard for myself. I chose to work 100-hour weeks. I chose to charge the bare minimum, and therefore I barely got by and continued to struggle financially. It wasn't until I hired a coach and started doing some inner work, that I realized my limiting beliefs and destructive patterns were keeping me in the struggle. The struggle was real because I made it real. Does that sound familiar for you?

The way I see it, you have a choice. You can stay committed to being broke, to struggling, to doing mediocre work because, for some messed-up, twisted reason, you think you deserve to suffer. Maybe you've told yourself it's part of the process. Maybe you've told yourself that business is hard, and most businesses fail. You probably have heard some kind of statistic like 9 of 10 businesses fail within 10 years.

Or you can choose to join the ranks of world-class entrepreneurs who grow their business while living a lifestyle that you used to be jealous of. You can decide to live the life that you have designed and create a business that is your vehicle for fulfillment, for self-actualization, and for your spiritual awakening. When a person becomes world-class, it's a decision, not an accident. Do you agree?

If you choose to put this book down, if you choose to not follow the steps in The Freedom Formula to becoming the Fearless Leader you know you are meant to be, you are choosing to continue to live in your old paradigm. You are choosing to continue to struggle. You'll continue to wander, to face rejection after rejection in sales, even when you lower your price so low that you're losing money! You'll continue to ask yourself, "Should I burn this heaping pile of crap I call my business and go back and get a real job, even though I know I'll hate it, but at least I'll be able to pay my rent." You'll continue to think that "it's so hard to find good people" and wonder why every person you hire, who seems good in the interview, ends up being a disaster.

But guess what? Because you are the cause and creator of your circumstances, you are completely in control of your ability to change them. I invite you now to make a decision. Decide if you are going to continue to struggle, or decide if you are committed to becoming world class, the best in your field, the best in your industry and your market, to become the best that you can be.

Decide that you are going to stop putting off living the life of your dreams, the life you deserve, the life of infinite possibilities. Decide that you are going to double down and make the right investments in your business that you have been putting off for "someday".

Decide that you, like every world-class athlete, like every top performer, are going to work with the best partners in the world. That you are going to hire the best people, even if they are expensive, because that's what you want your clients to do. Right?

Decide that you are going to raise the standards for whom you choose to spend your time with and whom you call your friend. And most importantly, raise your standards for you.

If you don't decide now, then when will you? If you don't choose to live life on your terms, then by whose terms are you living your life? If you don't decide to be great, are you willing to fade into the background and join the cult of mediocrity?

And you'll do all this by working fewer hours and having way more fun. Once you make these decisions, distractions fade away like background noise, and you cut down to the few essential projects and tasks. You know, "focus". That thing we all know we should be doing, but we end up saying, "yes" to so many distractions disguised as "opportunities". Focus requires decisiveness, and decisiveness comes from knowing what you really want. This book will show you how to have that, and the result is working few hours and having a much higher impact.

Look, I know what it's like to feel like you are going through the motions of life. To feel too tired and drained to have the energy to do what you know is necessary. I know what it's like to feel like a zombie from the moment you get out of bed, counting down the hours until you can get back in bed at night and turn off the lights. I know what it's like to be working for the weekend. I know what it's like to avoid the pain of reality with food, with TV, with drugs. Just name your distraction. But there comes a moment in every person's life where they are given an opportunity to make a decision to be great or to stay stuck. The decision is yours. If you're committed to the struggle, please, put this book down, because it will only make you angry. Trust me, there are better ways to spend your time. Just turn on the TV, just turn on social media, and let that dopamine and cortisol flow through your brain and stay on the hamster wheel of addiction.

This book is not meant to be easy; it's meant to be effective. I am not going to complicate this anymore than it needs to be. I'm actually going to make it extremely simple. I'm going to be with you every step of the way, and I'm going to invite you to call me at any point. Here's my cell phone number +1-613-292-1159 (Canada). You can send me a text right now to let me know that you are reading this and that you have made it this far in the book.

Look, I believe in you. You just need to believe in yourself. If you have decided now is your time, then I am so excited for you. I am so honoured to be your guide to becoming a Fearless Leader. Let's do this.

Claim your free gifts at www.smallbiztrap.com.

Chapter 2

The #1 Reason Why Small Business Owners Stay Trapped

Donna, a real estate agent, had come to me for advice on sales. When we first sat down she told me that she was new to the business as a second career and that she was concerned about competing against young energetic real estate agents and seasoned professionals. She knew she wanted to grow her sales, but when it came to defining who her ideal client was, she was unclear. The first step in the Freedom Formula to become a Fearless Leader is Clarity. This is where you get clear on who you want to serve and how you want to serve them. Next, you will get clear on what your strengths and passions are. If you don't have this clarity, you're likely to wander from job to job, contract to contract, never feeling fully aligned to your mission.

You may be thinking that you already know what I do, and your business is working fine. Or maybe you feel that you've invested so much into what you are currently doing, that you can't afford to change course. Don't worry, this is about getting clearer and may require only a few subtle shifts to really boost your results

Getting clear means really understanding what success means to you, knowing how to get paid to do what you love, knowing the challenges your ideal customer is facing, and understanding what comes easily to you.

Donna told me that she used to be a nurse in the maternity ward, helping young couples through the experience of birthing a new baby. She told me how she had a calming effect on the couple throughout the labour, and she would spend extra time with them after the baby was born to help them wrap their head around the idea of being responsible for a new baby.

So, we looked at how that skill set translated into real estate sales. We realized that she is an expert in "emotional responsibility" and the transition of going from the carefree life of being a young couple to the responsibility of being a parent. This is perfect for first time homebuyers!

She made the decision to market herself as a first-time homebuyer expert, and she used her personal story to connect with young couples. It worked so well, she called me a few months later saying that she hit her annual sales goals in three months! Of course, she took clients of all types, but because she made a choice to position herself as an expert in one niche, it gave her the clarity to know how to market herself, and it attracted her ideal client.

You may feel that choosing one focus in business means you can't do business in other areas. Not true. Choose one thing to be known for, and then feel free to accept any business that you feel is a good fit for you and your customer. For example, I focus my marketing on sales for small businesses, but once we start working together, they hire me for public speaking training, time management training, and what amounts to life coaching. They are all tied together, but it's very hard to market them all at the same time.

Or you may be afraid to make a decision because you are worried about what other people will think. Here's an important insight. You know how you worry about what other people think about you? Guess what? All those other people are worried about what other people think of them. They are not even thinking about you. And even if they are, it doesn't really matter.

This chapter is about creating a crystal clear image of what you really want your life and your business to look like. This is the most important step. Without knowing what you want your life and business to look like, there is no amount of strategies or tactics that are going to help you get to where you want to go, because you don't know where you want to go.

I was out having breakfast with a mentor of mine, when he asked me what my greatest challenge in business was. I told him that I wanted to grow my sales. He said, "By how much?" I told him, "I don't know." He then reached into his pocket and pulled out a quarter and slid it across the table. "There you go. You've increased your sales. Now, would you like to be more specific?"

Vague goals produce vague results. Clarity creates focus, power, and momentum. Let's get you super clear on the results you really want. I find that it helps to breakdown your business and lifestyle goals into the following ten categories.

BUSINESS	**LIFESTYLE**
Money	Health
Clients	Friends
Business	Growth
Team	Fun
	Location
	Family

Answer each of the following questions with crystal clarity. For example, when you see the questions "How much money am I committed to making each month?" instead of writing "lots and lots of money" you would write something like "I commit to making over $10,000 per month, profit, for 10 months, and I will take two months off to travel each year, which will give me a net profit of over $100,000."

Be specific.

Instead of saying "I want to be in the best shape of my life" write "I am committed to working out 30 minutes per day for 5 days a week and to recording my workouts in my journal, no matter what."

Get ridiculously specific.

Money

I am committed to paying myself _____ dollars per month, no matter what.

My business deserves reinvestment, so I am committing to making more money than I need to pay myself, so I have a healthy profit margin. The gross* sales I commit to each month is _____, no matter what.

A portion of all of the money I earn is mine to keep and invest. Therefore, I commit to saving and investing _____ % of my gross sales.

*Gross is the money that comes in, before expenses.

Clients

I love my clients because _____.

My ideal client is _____.

My best clients pay me _____ per _____ for doing _____.

I say "no" to clients who want to hire me if _____.

Business

The milestone accomplishments in my business over the next three years are _____.

What makes me most proud of my business is _____.

The parts of my business that I most enjoy working on are _____.

The parts of my business that I would rather empower someone else to support me with are _____.

My growth goals for my business are _____.

Team

The people who support my business are _____.

The various roles of my contractors, consultants, employees, or suppliers are _____.

I describe my ideal support team as _____.

Health

I take full responsibility for my health, and I am committed to creating optimal health for myself. I define optimal health as _____.

My body is the temple for my mind and soul, and I feed it the best possible nutrition. My nutritional commitments are _____, no matter what.

My energy drives my results. I commit to keeping high energy by doing _____, _____, and _____.

Friends

I love my friends because _____.

My definition of great friendship is _____.

I am a great friend by being _____ and doing _____.

The ideal amount of time invested per week with friends is _____.

Growth

I spend _____ time reading per day.

I attend _____ educational conferences or seminars per year _____.

I challenge myself to grow by _____.

Fun

I invest _____ time per _____ having fun.

The activities I have the most fun doing are _____.

I incorporate fun into my work by _____.

Location

My ideal home is _____.

My ideal working environment is _____.

I travel to _____.

I travel _____ times per _____.

Family

I invest _____ time with my family every _____.

The activities I love to do with family are _____.

My significant other and I are committed to _____.

Remember to be as specific as possible, as if you were placing a custom order for your ideal life and business. This is the reality you are creating.

Now that you are clear on your ideal life and business, let me show you a model for getting paid to do what you love. My mentor, Sunjay Nath, showed me this model when I was starting in my professional speaking career. I continue to use this model to support my clients in having more fun with their business, and it helps me think through the ways I can create more value doing the things I love. It's called the M.A.P. To The Money Spot.

One of my favourite creative business/lifestyle questions is "How do I get paid to do what I love?" You may be thinking that work is one thing, and having fun is something you do when you're not working. Or perhaps you have been working so many hours, hustling, that it feels like you no longer love what you do. But if you want your sales to increase, loving what you do will help you attract more clients.

There are three elements required to get paid to do what you love and follow your M.A.P. To The Money Spot. Those three elements are Market, Aptitude, and Passion.

M stands for MARKET. Market is what people pay for to solve problems. The bigger the problem, the more valuable its solution. And the more you will get paid. The market is made up of customers. Customers are the people that have the problem that they want to pay you to solve. Who you choose as your customer is a big part of your experience, positive or negative, and business. I recommend working with customers you love. My measure is, "Would I want them in my home for dinner?" If not, it's not a good fit for me. I need to love my customers. So think about who you would love to serve and ask them this question: What is your biggest challenge right now? What keeps you up at night? Their answer to that question is the most valuable problem you can solve.

A stands for APTITUDE. Aptitude is your skills. Do what you are good at, because your customer deserves the best. Ask yourself this question: "What is easy for me that is hard for most people?" You might call this your gift or your talent. What is one thing that you could become the best at in your field? Your customer deserves the best.

P stands for PASSION. Passion is what you love. It's what you look forward to doing. And you'll notice, that when you do what you love, one hour feels like five minutes. But, when you do something you hate, five minutes feels like an hour. So ask yourself this question: What do I do that puts me in the zone and in my flow, and makes time speed up? I remember working at the hardware store when I was 16 years old, and I would play a game to wait as long as I could to look at the clock. One day it was 4:55 p.m., and my shift ended in five minutes. I waited and waited until what I thought would be 5 o'clock, and when I looked back at the clock, it still said 4:55 p.m. It was a digital clock. I thought it was broken. In fact, it was just such a slow time for me because I was so not passionate about the work.

If you only have two of the three elements, then you won't get paid to do what you love. If you have Aptitude and Passion, you have a hobby, and you are not getting paid. If there is a Market and you are Passionate that is a dream. You won't get paid because you don't have the necessary skills, but that is the easiest problem to solve because skills are learnable. If you have a Market and Aptitude, you may be unfortunate enough to find a soul sucking job, where you get paid well to do work that you are good at, but hate doing. It is my mission to free people from their soul sucking jobs and find work that they are passionate about and find their Money Spot.

In order to become a Fearless Leader, you must know what you want in every area of your business and life. The first step to getting what you want is knowing what you want. I suggest you get clear on what you want your lifestyle to look like first, so that you can design your business to facilitate your ultimate lifestyle. If the design of your life and business are not aligned, you will have to sacrifice one or the other. I much prefer you have your cake and eat it too.

Clarity Means:

- Knowing what success means to you

- Knowing how to get paid to do what you love

- Knowing the challenges your ideal client is facing

- Knowing what comes easily to you

Claim your free gifts at www.smallbiztrap.com.

Chapter 3

Turn Your Most Overlooked Resource into Massive Profits

I used to think I was not creative. And you may feel the same way. Growing up, I focused on math and science. I made top grades in the analytical classes, because I could study and memorize the right answers. Classes like art, painting, or photography always intimidated me because there was no right answer. It made me so frustrated.

So, I decided I wasn't creative. It wasn't until I changed my definition of creativity that I realized that not only am I creative, but also it is one of my superpowers. It is your superpower, too. It is how you can acheive your goals faster than you ever thought possible.

In this chapter, you will learn how to use the most overlooked resource in business called Creativity. You will learn how to get things done faster, easier, and have fun doing it. In business, the result of applying Creativity is more sales, more fun, and less work.

Making Business Easy and Fun

Samantha is a lawyer. She loves to give and receive gifts. One of her clients loves to cook, and her birthday was coming up, so she ordered a special Japanese chef's knife and had her client's name engraved on the knife, along with the words "Happy Birthday". When her client received the gift, she was so touched and said it was one of the most thoughtful gifts she had ever received. She has been a loyal customer for years following, and has referred many clients. Every time she has a friend over for dinner, she tells the story of the knife. Great marketing! That's Creativity.

Sylvia, a marketing consultant, loves to cycle. Whenever she can, she meets her clients on her bike and shows up in her biking gear. It allows her to do what she loves and differentiates her from other consultants who insist on wearing professional business attire. It creates conversation, and she often ends up inviting clients to join her on her weekend bike rides, which builds the relationship while she gets to do what is fun for her.

By incorporating fun into business, work doesn't feel like work anymore, and your clients get to see the side of you that is fully engaged and enthusiastic. This is very attractive and will result in more loyal customers and more sales. It's less work because relationship development becomes a natural by-product of having fun with your clients, and you don't need to stress over complicated marketing campaigns. You just ask yourself, "How can I have fun with my current and future clients?" More sales, more fun, less work.

You Are Creative

Now, let's define Creativity in a way that will show you that you are a creative being. Creativity is not limited to the ability to draw, or paint, or sing, although those are all creative activities. Creativity is the act of creating. It is having an idea and making it real. You are creative when you decide what to wear in the morning. You are creative when you open up the refrigerator and throw together a meal from odd ingredients. You are creative when you are running out of time and have to find a way to get it done no matter what.

Creativity comes from questions. What should I wear today? What can I cook from these ingredients and make for dinner? How can I get this done in the next 15 minutes (when you thought you would need two hours)?

In business, Creativity comes from questions such as these: How can I have more fun with my clients? How can I provide ten times more value than I am currently providing? What would my product or service look like if my client were paying ten times what they are currently paying? How can I make my offer unique from all of my competitors? How can I decrease my costs and increase the quality of my product? How can I have more fun with my clients?

Questions focus the mind, and they help generate creative answers. Asking different kinds of questions can lead to different types of results.

Let's look at how you can use Creativity to overcome a limiting belief. "I can't afford a new car" is a belief. "How can I get a new car in a way that is fun and easy and doesn't cost me any money?" Now that is a great question that will spark Creativity.

Knowing myself, and my gifts, my strength and my passion, I am immediately going to my training offerings and my speaking expertise as my tool to create value. So I think, maybe I could call a car dealership and ask them if they want sales training for their staff, in exchange for a lease on one of their vehicles. Or, I could ask a friend if I could use his car while he's out of the country. Or I can ask myself, which friends of mine have an extra car that they never use, and what can I offer them that would feel valuable enough for them to let me borrow their car? Or maybe I could lease a new car and sign up to be an Uber driver for the payments. And I could continue to come up with more ideas to answer the question, how can I get a new car, even if I don't have the money? And adding the part about making it easy and fun is a bonus. But if I stayed stuck in my original belief that I can't afford a new car, I would never even try to come up with ideas. Ask questions to turn on the creative juices.

Putting Creativity to Work

Below I'm going to give you some examples of clients who have turned on their Creativity and what it's done for their businesses.

I have a client who, when she came to me, believed she was too busy to exercise. She worked long hours and spent much of her time driving from one client to the other. She is a life coach and believed that in order to be effective, she needed to work in person, face-to-face. And because her clients were paying her, she thought it was only fair for her to drive so it was convenient for them, even if it wasn't convenient for her.

We started playing with reframing the belief into a question. Instead of I'm too busy to exercise we created a question: "How can I make time for exercise, in a way that is fun and easy, that would actually create more value for my clients?" So this is what we came up with. She offered to have walking coaching sessions, which her clients absolutely loved. They would come and meet at her house and then go for a walk together.

The result was quite astounding. By getting out of their office or the house, they actually got more value because they were with my client in her element. By walking and getting fresh air, they felt more energized and creative. My client, the life coach, got to spend more time with her clients and less time in her car driving from one client to the next. For other clients she offered to do phone coaching session instead of face-to-face, and the value added was that she would record the phone call. She decided to do her phone calls while she was walking on a nature trail instead of being cooped up in her office. Again, walking, and her clients found the phone calls convenient too because they didn't have to worry about where they would have to be during the coaching calls.

She has even had meetings with prospective clients at the gym. She found a way to have her cake and eat it too: to be with her clients while doing the other things she enjoys.

As I mentioned in the introduction, I used repeated a cycle of start business, sell business, travel 5 times to travel to 24 countries before I was 21 years old. Each time I would end up back home, broke, with no business. And then it dawned on me that I needed to ask myself a different question.

The question started off as this: How can I run a business where I don't need to settle in order to travel? It turned into another question that excited me: How do I get paid to travel? I thought of ideas like becoming a photographer, or a writer, or a businessman who works for an international company. And that one question led to more questions that eventually led to this one: How do I get paid to do what I love?

From my time in the high school theater and on the high school speech team, and later in college improv comedy trips, I knew I loved to perform on stage. I even had the opportunity to perform at an improv show in New York City with Amy Poehler and Horatio Sans from Saturday Night Live. I had also developed a love for entrepreneurship and personal development, so I thought it would be perfect for me to become a motivational speaker. I could travel, perform, and share my gifts and wisdom with the world.

In a way, that's what I do today. I have been delivering corporate training since 2010 with Learning Tree International, eventually becoming their top-rated trainer in the world out of a crew of 721 trainers, and working with global brands like the United Nations, the federal governments of Canada and United States, companies like Citibank, Coca-Cola, L'Oreal, and many of the Fortune 500 companies. And while I went into those engagements under the guise of corporate trainer, for me, it was really an opportunity to transform people's lives on a personal level, while performing three solid days of stand-up comedy and improv. And I was paid to do what I love: travelling and performing. It was a dream come true.

Ask Yourself These Questions

I know, in your business, not everything is fun, and some things are "just the way it is." Your clients have certain expectations and your industry has certain norms that don't allow for Creativity. But imagine if you started asking yourself different questions, such as how can I make this more easy and fun? How can I work less and create more value for my client? If you start with those questions, what creative ideas do you think you will discover?

I used to love travelling for work, going out to train and consult across North America, but when my first child Ruby was born, my priorities shifted to being at home. My definition of success changed.

With new priorities I needed to change the questions I was asking. The new question became, how do I get paid to do what I love, maximize my impact on the world, while being the best possible father and husband, and while being at home as much as possible? Be specific with your questions and you'll get specific answers. You try it. Ask yourself the question, as specifically as possible, and see what kind of answer comes up for you. Your question might be "how do I double my income while working less and having more fun?"

More Time with the Horses

"How do I only work with my favourite clients, make as much money as I'm making today, while spending more time with my horses?"

My client, Maggie, has about 600 clients in her small accounting firm. She's actually my accountant. I love her. And we were talking one day, and I asked her—as I often ask people, because I love to know about people's dreams—where do you see yourself in five years? She described to me an ideal life, spending time with her two horses, living at her lake house, and only working with her favourite clients, with mostly remote work from her lake house, over the phone, and over the Internet. She could do that client work from anywhere in the world. And then came the powerful question, "So why don't you do that now?" Then came the fear, the limiting beliefs. "Well, I don't know if I can afford it. I don't know if my clients will be interested in working with me over the phone. A lot of my clients like to come into my downtown office and sit with me face-to-face." So we kept talking and came up with a simple strategy.

The strategy emerged as we asked questions, such as this: how could you easily remove your least favourite clients from your client list and make even more profits? How could you arrange it so that all of your clients are willing to work with you remotely, and the ones who want face-to-face meetings could meet with someone else?

So here was the simple plan we came up with. Raise her prices by 25 percent, and increase the service level with a quarterly one-on-one call. Those calls will be done over the phone, and face-to-face meetings where possible, if her clients were willing to go to her lake house. Anyone who did not want to pay the higher rates, would be referred to a partner accountant whom she knows and trusts and believes will serve her clients well. Out of 300 clients 100 chose to work with the other accountant, and 150 decided to stay with her, at the higher price point, with the higher service level. The remaining 50 decided to take their business elsewhere.

The result was, she had about half of the workload she had before, and she automatically had her favourite clients, because the ones who stuck with her loved her and didn't want to work with anyone else. And, by the way, they loved the strategy calls once per quarter. As for the 100 clients who went to work with the other accountant, that accountant is paying an ongoing referral fee and gets ongoing support from Maggie during the transition. She made sure that each one of her former clients was taken care of and treated well, and she explained all the little nuances of their preferences so that they would continue to get the same special treatment they always got from her at the original price.

Maggie is working less, making the same amount of money, working from her lake house, and spending time with her horses. This is a simple strategy. Basically raise your prices, and offer your clients a choice to stick with you, or give them a decent option if they choose not to. Just because it's simple, doesn't make it easy. It was scary for Maggie, because she thought her clients would pushback and get upset, thinking she was greedy. She thought her clients would leave her, and the business she spent over a decade building would come falling down. She had to face her own beliefs about self-worth. Who am I to charge this much? My clients will leave me and go somewhere cheaper.

You may choose to experiment with a few clients to see their reaction to a price increase. Change always requires Courage on some level, because Courage is action in spite of fear and uncertainty.

So far in this chapter you've seen that we all have Creativity within us, and that it's really all about asking the right kinds of questions. For Maggie—she asked the question "How can I make more money, work less, and spend more time with my horses?" Then she came up with creative solutions for a business that made her feel free instead of trapped.

Now it's your turn. Write down some questions using this framework. How can I (create a desired result) while (using my strengths and passions) without (suffering)? For example, "How can I get one new client per week by attending events that I enjoy attending without feeling uncomfortable when I network?"

Limiting Beliefs

We can ask ourselves questions and start coming up with some pretty great solutions, but those solutions aren't going to help us if we're held back by old beliefs. Old beliefs have the power to prevent you from seeing possibilities and to stop you in your tracks. But if we start to listen to those old beliefs with a sense of curiosity and ask, "Is that really true?" we can start to replace them, and then we can truly set ourselves free.

You may have grown up, like me, believing that business is risky, that you should play it safe, and that asking for money is bad. If you believe asking for money is bad, it's really hard to make a sale! I have worked through many beliefs like the ones I just listed, and I'm constantly finding more beliefs that no longer serve me and are ready for an upgrade.

At my retreat, Mastermind Spa (www.mastermindspa. com), I pass out rubber bands for my attendees to wear around their wrist. The rubber band is a reminder to listen to your "self talk". And when you hear yourself saying something that is not loving towards yourself, something that is not an expansive belief, but instead a limiting belief, then you pull on the rubber band and snap it against your wrist. That gives you the conditioning to give a small punishment when you have a limiting belief, and give you a moment to replace it with a supportive and expansive positive one.

If ever you think, I can't do it, you pull the rubber band, snap, ouch! And replace it with an expansive question like: How can I do it in a way that's easy and fun? My clients would never pay that much—snap—what can I offer my clients that they would gladly pay that much, and feel like they're getting an incredible deal for? While having fun and doing it in a way that is easy for me?

"I'm no good with technology. I'm a computer idiot." Pull the rubber band, snap! Replace it with, "How can I learn how to be great with technology, in a way that is easy and fun for me?" I've learned how to do all sorts of things. I can learn how to be great with technology. Technology is my friend.

How can I get paid to travel? Do something valuable when I'm on the road. I could do my coaching calls on the road. What can I do that would be super valuable? What is the most valuable creation I could make while traveling?

Questions have led me to create my program called Business from the Beach. Actually, I say I created that program, but really, my clients created that program. At the end of my first Mastermind Spa retreat (www.mastermindspa. com) I made an offer. I said I'm going to rent a big house, on the beach, and work with a few of my favourite clients on their business from the beach. I offered it for $5000 (today I offer it at $15,000) and right away two people purchased it on the spot, without having to know any details. They were happy to pay.

I came home that night at midnight, and woke up my wife, and told her, sweetheart, we're going to Trinidad and Tobago, and our clients are paying for it. She was excited, and confused, and said let's talk about it in the morning. I couldn't sleep. I was so excited. I had created an entire retreat and program simply by asking the question, who wants to work on their business from the beach with me?

Make offers. If your clients are interested, they will tell you what they want, instead of your trying to figure out all the details. Let your clients be partners in your Creativity, in developing how you are going to serve and support them. They understand their challenges better than you do. Just be willing to be creative and ask expansive questions.

How can I serve and support you in a deeper way? What would be the most valuable thing I can do for you? What would be a dream come true solution that I could provide for you? All these questions creatively allow you to provide your clients more money. It's up to you to find a way to do it in the way that's most fun and easy for you. Just ask yourself, how can I get my clients the results that they want in a way that is fun and easy for me.

Here's another great question that can help you see how

you can raise the quality of your offering while significantly raising the price. What would my service look like if I charge 10 times what I'm charging now?

Growing up, I never paid for haircuts. My mom cut my hair on the back porch, because, as my dad would say, paying for a haircut was a waste of money. We had the same policy about haircuts as we did with mowing the lawn. Let it grow as long as the neighbours don't complain, and then cut it as short as possible. So I would let my hair grow out to a curly puppy Afro, and then would shave it down nearly to my scalp.

Even when I went off to college, I still felt that paying for a haircut was a waste of money. So I bought myself the cheapest electric shaver I could find, and I shaved my own head over the bathroom sink. Every few months, I would buzz it down to nothing, and then I let it grow back out to an Afro. From time to time I would go in and get a $10 haircut at the Great Clips. The service was not friendly. The hairstylists would act like it was inconvenient when anyone walked in, because it was interrupting their day. At the end of the haircut, I paid my $10, gave a one-dollar tip, and would be on my way. That was my experience of paying for a haircut.

In 2009, after I started making a bit of money, it had been almost a year since I had cut my hair. I met the owner of Saab Salon, a man named Frank Saab, like the Swedish car. He had beautiful hair. He was buff and tan: a real man's man. While talking, and he looked at my hair and said, "My friend, you need to come and see me. You have beautiful hair, but you're not treating it like your hair deserves." He reached into his Italian leather man bag, and handed me a coupon for $25 off a haircut. My first thought was, $25 off? Geez, how much is a haircut? He said $50. I said, "$50?" That's five times more than I paid for my last haircut. It must be pretty amazing. Notice how higher prices create the expectation that the service will be better?

I just had to see what a $50 hair cut was like. So I set the appointment and showed up at the salon the next week.

It. Was. Amazing!

I was greeted by name, given a cappuccino while I waited, and had a warm hair wash and aromatherapy face massage. When it was time for my hair cut, I was in such a good mood from the royal treatment. Frank looked at my hair like Michelangelo would look at a block of marble he was preparing to sculpt. Like a true professional, he told me about my face shape and hair texture. When he was finished cutting my hair, he recommended a few products specific to my hair type. When it was all over, I rang up my order at the cash register, gave the $25 off coupon, and decided I would give a $25 tip because I was so happy with the service.

Two weeks later I got the credit card bill. I hadn't even paid attention to the bill at the salon, but when I saw the number on the bill, it was $160 dollars! My first thought was, "that was totally worth it!" So how did I go from $10 haircuts to $160 haircuts? Frank provided way more value and an unforgettable experience.

Now it's your turn. Here is a creative exercise to help you think about what you could offer at significantly higher prices than what you are offering now. The question is "What would your service look like if you charged 10 times what you are charging now?" Think about that, and you will have ideas for creating more value for your clients.

Now you know that Creativity is simply asking better questions and generating answers. Applying this to your life will not only increase the value of your business, but also increase the happiness in your life.

Creativity:

- Creates more fun in your business

- Is an act of creation—have an idea and make it real

- Comes from asking questions

Claim your free gifts at www.smallbiztrap.com.

Chapter 4

Commit and Grow Rich

The Fearless Leaders knows what she wants (Clarity), finds ways to get what she wants, even when it seems impossible (Creativity), and has decided that she is going to make it happen, no matter what (Commitment).

Commitment is what makes you unstoppable. When you have a revenue target that you decide you are going to hit, you don't stop if you fall short. You just keep going. To quote Vishen Lakhiani in his book, *The Code Of The Extraordinary Mind* you become "unfuckwithable".

My client Jennifer, who works with municipalities helping them with group buying contracts, had been working on landing a deal with a municipality for over a year. She would phone every single week and stop by the city hall at least once per month. After four rejected presentations, she was finally given the opportunity to submit a proposal, and it was accepted. After she got the deal, she asked one of the council members why they finally changed their minds, and he told her, "We figured if you were this committed to our contract, then you'll be as committed in everything you do for us." Persistence pays off.

Another of my clients, Ashley, has a strict rule to not work on the weekends, because she is committed to family time. She doesn't attend events, she doesn't take client calls, and she doesn't work on her business on the weekend. If she ever makes a conscious exception, she increases her family time during the week.

When there isn't a commitment, your results suffer. One all-too-common lack of commitment is not being committed to taking care of your health with the proper diet, sleep, exercise, and self-care. When the client's needs come before your needs, your health suffers and ultimately deteriorates. I know personally from gaining weight and losing sleep as I built my business, that the only solution is to get committed and stay committed.

A lack of commitment to ongoing sales activity means that when business is good, you stop reaching out to prospects, and then your sales pipeline dries up. A commitment to ongoing sales activity means a healthy flow of new business. Get specific about what the commitment is; otherwise your results will suffer.

Commitment creates clear boundaries of when to say "yes" or "no", which ultimately gives you the freedom to do what you want without feeling obligated to please others. Without commitment, you fall into the trap of reacting to other people's demands and putting your own goals on the back burner.

It's time to make a decision. Decide to commit. Without commitment, you are doomed to wander aimlessly, and suffer from Shiny Object Syndrome. You may feel that committing to one path steals away your freedom, but in fact, it is the exact opposite. When you know what you want and you decide you are going after it, everything non-essential falls away, and you reclaim enormous amounts of energy and focus to pursue only that which is fully aligned to your mission.

If you've made it this far, that tells me you are committed

to understanding this process. You deserve to recognize yourself for your perseverance and dedication. If you haven't taken the time to get the clarity you deserve, go back and answer the questions in chapter 3.

Are you committed to really changing your life and your business forever? Are you committed to doubling, tripling, or quadrupling your sales? Or are you committed to staying stuck? Are you committed to making work easy and fun, or are you committed to the struggle? It doesn't have to be hard. But you do need to make a decision. What lies beyond the decision may be scary. In fact it is absolutely scary, because it is the unknown. We have evolved to fear the unknown, because there are dangers lurking behind those questions, our caveman mind tells us. What if; what if.

It is interesting to note the root of the word "decision", coming from the Latin *decisio*, which literally means "to cut off" or "to cut". It has the same root word as the words "incision" and "scissors". They all mean to cut. When you make a decision, what happens to the possibilities not chosen? If you don't cut off those other possibilities, they continue to nag at you, to drain you, to suck at your psychic energy. True decision is fully committing to moving forward in action. And when you do make the decision, it is important to take action as quickly as possible.

Tony Robbins is quoted as saying; "Never leave the scene of a decision without taking action." When you make a decision as you are reading this book, I encourage you to take action right on the spot. Make that phone call; send that email; send that text message right away. That makes your decision permanent. If you decide to let go of a client or staff member, write an email immediately that holds you accountable. If you are committed to a sales goal higher than ever before, then send an email out to your team and state the goal publicly. If you are going to invest in a training program or new software, then take a few minutes now and just do it! Don't think, just act. Too much thinking allows fear to creep in.

In my retreats, I invite my participants to make a mind map of all of their ongoing commitments in their life and business. They take a large piece of paper and fill it with a web of words like Rotary club and gym membership, family time, TV time, doctor visits, clients, projects, association memberships, committees, marketing initiatives, events, and all of the other commitments that fill their days and weeks and months in their life. Then I ask, "What commitments can you let go of to make room for new commitments?"

You may decide to leave a club that you have been a member of for too long. You may decide to step down from a Board of Directors, or decide that your weekly visit to the pub could be a monthly visit. One of my students decided that she would organize a carpool to take her kids to hockey instead of driving them to every single practice. She told me that decision saved her 20 hours a week. What would you do with an extra 20 hours a week?

How could you apply this in your business? What areas of commitment could you reduce or eliminate?

Doing this exercise in your business is a great way to apply the 80/20 rule. The 80/20 rule states that 80 percent of your results come from 20 percent of your efforts. If you could clearly see on a single sheet of paper all of the efforts you are making in your business and life, you would be able to pick out the critical few areas of focus that make up a majority of your positive results. It's likely that if you have 10 clients, 80 percent of your revenue is coming from two clients and 20 percent of your revenue is coming from the other 8 clients. So you could let go of some or all of the 8 clients that make up 20 percent of your revenue and focus your efforts on getting more clients like the two clients that account for 80 percent of your revenue.

So in this exercise, I ask people to formulate the language that makes the decision real. For example, when I first did this exercise myself, I was a member of five different clubs, and I was the president of two of those clubs. My calendar was full of club meetings and conference calls, and not enough time was dedicated to my business and my family. I decided I would take back 10 to 15 hours per week by leaving three of those clubs that were not serving me at the highest level anymore.

I formulated the language for the email that would renegotiate the commitment. It went something like this.

Dear club members, upon recent review of my commitments, workload, and schedule, I have realized that I can no longer engage with this club at the level that I committed to. Instead of trying to fit it all in and doing a half assed job, I have decided to end my membership. I love you all very much and appreciate so much the role you have played in my life in the past few years. I am sure we will stay friends and I wish you all great success. Let's arrange for a smooth transition of my responsibilities. If anyone would be interested in taking on a few new projects for this club please, please reach out to me.

Talk about a weight off of my shoulders. So much time opened up in my calendar, I was able to do the things that I've been putting off, in my health, my family, and my business. I invite you to do the same thing. Look at where your time goes on your calendar. Are you giving up your time to projects or commitments and relationships that are not serving you at the highest level? Would the future successful you still keep these commitments? And if not when are you going to let them go? If not now, then when? To become the higher version of you, start acting like the higher version of you right now.

If this sounds like a good fit for you, I would encourage you to request an invitation to one of my upcoming retreats. Shoot me an email at majeed@majeedm.com or check out www.mastermindspa.com for details. This is the fastest way I know of to create your ultimate lifestyle, experience more freedom, and become a Fearless Leader!

Decision-Making

Why is decision-making hard? Because we are afraid we are going to make the wrong decision. We don't trust ourselves. Let me ask you something, when did you stop trusting yourself? Why don't you trust yourself? My guess is at some point you made a decision that you decided was a bad decision. Or someone else told you that you made a bad decision, and you believed him or her.

Trust me, I have had my fair share of these types of experiences. Such as when I bought that purple shirt, and my dad said it was a stupid purchase, I felt like I made a bad decision with my money. And for years and years, and still at some level today, I am afraid of money decisions. But what if every decision you made was the right decision for you in that moment. What if every decision you made had always led you to some valuable outcome. Hasn't there been something good from every decision you have ever made? The only bad decision is not making a decision at all.

Trust Your Gut

Trust your gut. Trust your intuition, because when you trust your gut, you really trust yourself. The subconscious mind is comparing all past experiences to your current experience. Your subconscious mind, or your gut, gives you infinite wisdom. You just have to listen. Think about the times you followed your gut, and you were right. Think about the times you ignored your gut and paid the price. So often we know the answer already. It's just scary. So we stay stuck, because stuck is familiar and taking action, making a decision, moving forward, is a scary step into the unknown. The familiar suffering feels safer than stepping into the unknown.

Don't be "realistic". Realistic, is playing safe, is living in old paradigms. Throw away "realistic" and embrace boldness. Fortune favours the bold. Take bold action. Take action in spite of fear, in spite of uncertainty, and you will have no regrets in this life. Take bold action when it comes to inviting a prospective client to work with you. Help them make their decision now, and close the deal boldly. Take bold action when investing in yourself and your business. Hire the best coach you can find, not the one you feel is in your budget. Hire the best possible team members to support you. Be bold.

Ask yourself, "What is one beautiful, bold step I can take right now?" I am here with you as you are reading, I believe in you, and I support your bold step. Why not take that step right now? Go! If you're not sure what to do, pick up the phone and call a past client and ask them what their challenges are right now. The easiest way to grow your business is to call on past clients for repeat business and referrals. But it takes Courage because you need to overcome the fear of rejection.

Right about now you might be playing the game of the

worrier called "the What If game". What if it doesn't work? What if it is a waste of my time? What if I lose money? What if I lose customers? What if people don't like it? What if people don't like me? What if? What if? The secret to taking massive decisive action is to stop thinking and start doing.

You don't need to play the "What If" game. But if you really want to, I invite you to play the "What If" game, but in the opposite direction. What if this transforms my life and my business for the better? What if this makes me more money than I've ever made? What if this has a huge impact on the lives of the people I serve? What if this makes all the difference? What if this works out even better than I thought it would?

I trained a financial advisor, Chris, to overcome his fear of making cold calls. Before we worked together, he didn't want to make the calls because he thought "What if I'm bothering them with my call?" and "What if they complain about me calling them?" We replaced that with "What if they are looking for a financial advisor?" and "What if your call is the friendliest call they receive all day?" and "What if they refer you to someone who is looking for a financial advisor?" Those better questions are all Chris needed to fuel his calls. He started making 100 calls per day and enjoyed it. He quickly became in the top 1 percent of the company because he was able to look at cold calling with a much better attitude than most of his colleagues.

Goals

One element of the decisions you have to make right now is the decision about what your goal is. Anyone who has journeyed into personal development knows that goals are at the heart of your progress. Should I do this or should I do that? The answer lies in what your goal is. There's a classic acronym for goal setting called S.M.A.R.T. goals. Specific, Measurable, Attainable, Realistic, and Time bound.

Specific: Be so clear that anyone would know exactly what you mean.

Measurable: How will you measure once you have gotten there? How do you know that you have achieved your goal? If it's measurable, you will be able to know when you're halfway there or when you're 25 percent of the way or when you're 10 percent of the way there, which helps you make a plan and set milestones.

Attainable: It needs to be possible to attain your goal, otherwise your mind will tell you it is impossible, and you will sabotage yourself.

Relevant: It fits into your greater life plan, life purpose, and it aligns to your values. It must be important to you and be relevant. This is where you ask yourself, is this goal for me, or is this a goal I'm setting to please someone else?

Time-bound: There is a specific date attached to it. I recommend a specific date instead of a period of time. For example, January 1, 2020 is better than in the next three years. Because, in my experience, "in the next three years" seems to always be three years away. The goal has the habit of rolling forward whereas, when you have a specific date, you can set milestone goals and track your progress.

Now, there is an inherent flaw in goals. Let me show you.

I want you to say the following phrase out loud. Tonight I am going to have dinner. Certainly, say it out loud. Notice how it feels. Does it feel true? Now say the following phrase out loud. "Tonight, my goal is to have dinner". You see the difference? Can you feel it? What's the difference between the two phrases? The first one has certainty, and the next one, with the goal, has the feeling that it might happen if you really stretched, or maybe not. A goal feels just out of reach. You really need to stretch because it feels hard. It doesn't feel easy. So I invite you to convert your goals into commitments. Here's how you do that. Add the words "I will" to the beginning of your goal, and add the words "no matter what" to the end of your goals.

So instead of saying, "I want to make $100,000 a year," instead write, "I will make $100,000 between today's date and one year from now, no matter what." Can you feel the difference? That's the difference between a goal and a commitment. I invite you to commit to achieving these outcomes, no matter what.

- Commit to being a Fearless Leader.

- Commit to taking amazing care of yourself and setting the example for how others should treat you.

- Commit to loving your customers.

- Commit to helping your prospects make the decision to work with you (sales).

- Commit to getting out of your comfort zone, and do something that scares you (be specific).

You may feel the question "how?" coming up. How can I

achieve that goal? It feels impossible. I don't have time. I don't have the skills. I'm not certified. And the list goes on. What you will notice is that the universe conspires for you to realize your commitments, from the moment you decide it is going to happen, no matter what. Your friends and family know the difference between a dream, a desire, and a commitment. Commitment has the energy of, "You can help me, or you can get out of my way. I don't need your advice, but I will take your support." Look out people, here comes the Fearless Leader.

Let me give you some specific language that I think will help you on your path. You will find some distractions that come your way disguised as opportunities. Opportunities to joint venture, opportunities to get a coffee, opportunities to attend that event, but once you have decided on your goals/ commitments it will be easier for you to know that you should say no to almost everything, and say yes to a very few critical opportunities. The following will help you say no in a way that is gentle and respectful, and doesn't give away your power.

How to Say "No" to a Meeting Request

Thank you for your kind invitation to meet. I am fully committed to a number of projects that require my full attention, and unfortunately I have not created the space for new opportunities, like having a meeting with you. If there is a specific request you have, I invite you to send it to me by email or send me a short list of questions that we can discuss on a 9-minute phone call.

Or, thank you for thinking of me for this opportunity. I'm committed to my clients for now until the perceivable future, and I have not set time aside for new meetings. That said, if you would like to pay for a 60-minute strategy call with me, my rate is (insert your rate here). If this is important enough for you, and you are willing to make the investment, then I am happy to dedicate my full attention to your request. Thank you again for your email, and If there is a fit for us to move forward at this point, then I very much look forward to speaking with you.

How to Let Go of Old Connections

This has been a really hard one for me. I feel loyal to my friends and old business colleagues, but I know that some of the old relationships from my past do not fit who I have become. If there's a friend or colleague who brings you down, and you feel uncomfortable with them, then you must make the decision to stop spending time with them. When you get clear on who qualifies for you to spend your time with, you stop spending low quality time in low quality relationships. Improve the quality of your relationships and you will improve your business with better connections that better fit the direction you are heading.

Weeding out old contacts that no longer fit can be incredibly uplifting. I hope this language helps you. The next time they invite you to hang out, or come to the party, you could say something like this. "Dear friend, I have become so committed to my business and my life work, that I haven't made time to be with you. I have had to make difficult decisions, and one of them is to spend less time socializing. I hope you will understand that right now, at this point in my life, I am not making the time for lunches or parties, because I am so involved with my family and my business. I want you to know that I cherish the memories that we have, and I am grateful for all the experiences we shared. I hope you feel the same, and I wish you the best on your journey."

How to Say "No" to a Last-minute Request

Thank you for thinking of me. I wish I could help, but I don't have the bandwidth right now. What I can do is this...

Tidying Up

There's a book titled *The Life Changing Magic of Tidying Up*. I read this book, along with a few other books on minimalism, including the book *Essentialism*, which I also highly recommend. I picked it up when my first child, Ruby, was born. My wife and I were living in a 520 square-foot, one-bedroom apartment, and I knew I had to start de-cluttering to make space for the baby. Little did I know that the act of letting go of old stuff would transform my life and business.

Once I learned how to "tidy up" my house, by learning a simple way to decide whether or not to keep something, I applied the same principal to every element of my life and business. I started to cut projects that were not top priority. I erased all 10,000 contacts from my phone and added only 100 of my favourite clients and relationships. I simplified all of my client processes, and I have helped my clients do the same. One exercise that I take all of my clients through is to have them list their top 100 business relationships. This takes about 20 minutes and it creates incredible clarity and focus. You can double your sales by focusing on deepening relationships and serving these 100 people.

The Life Changing Magic of Tidying Up is a personal development book disguised as a house-cleaning tool. I'm going to share with you the one fundamental principle from this book that has had a radical impact on my life. The method, recommended by the author, for deciding on what to keep, and what to let go is simple and intuitive and shockingly effective. For each item you own, just ask, "Does this spark joy"? The answer will be abundantly clear on an intuitive level. If the answer is yes, keep it. If the answer is no, let it go. So simple. So effective. Try it!

You can de-clutter the objects in your life, the commitments of your life, the relationships of your life; you can even let go of the beliefs and thoughts in your mind. What remains is completely true to your authentic self.

Now apply this to your business. What are you doing in your business that you don't really love, maybe you think you "should" be doing it, but it doesn't actually spark joy.

Cathy owns a commercial interior design firm, and a retail furniture and residential interior design store. When we met, she had goals to open a second retail location in the same city and open a third retail location overseas in Aruba. The goal of opening two new stores within twelve months excited her, but when she was honest with herself, she knew it would lead her to a lifestyle of overwork and lack of focus. She "de-cluttered" her goals and decided to focus on growing her existing operations. Instantly she felt more energized and focused. Simplify to amplify.

Maybe there are clients you have been working with for a long time, but you dread speaking with them, so you try to avoid them. Guess what? It's time to let them go. Maybe you have been taking on projects that used to excite you but now bore you to tears. Let them go! The path to Fearless Leadership is paved with powerful decisions to let the old go to make room for the new.

Commitment:

- Makes you unstoppable and unfuckwithable

- Means you're going to make it happen no matter what

- Creates clear boundaries

- Help you make decisions

- Means you trust your gut

- Is the difference between "I will" and "I want"

Claim your free gifts at www.smallbiztrap.com.

Chapter 5

The Fearless Leader Habit That Turns Problems into Profit

Three areas that you can grow with Courage are investing in yourself, public speaking, and sales.

I remember sitting in a real estate investment seminar, listening to someone who called herself the rich mom. It was a play off of the popular real estate book, *Rich Dad Poor Dad*. She told a story that was very inspiring to me. At the time I wasn't a father. I was a broke, unemployed, immigrant in Canada, without a work visa. Since I couldn't legally be employed in Canada, my solution was to try my hand at real estate investment.

The presenter told the story of incredible courage. She told us how she had received a diagnosis that her son was ill and required medical attention that would cost hundreds of thousands of dollars. She was basically given the ultimatum by her doctor that if she didn't find a way to come up with hundreds of thousands of dollars, her son would die. Any parent at that point would have to choose to become a victim, or to cultivate levels of Courage never before seen. She got into massive action and started buying and flipping houses. Within a matter of months she had generated the money she needed to save her son. It was an incredible story, and I have been inspired by so many stories of Courage since then.

Having Courage in business means being uncomfortable (a lot), asking for the sale, and saying "no" to opportunities that don't fit your plan (Clarity). With Courage you feel less trapped in business because you know you can take massive action and change your circumstances at any time.

The first act of Courage I invite you to take is to raise your fees (even if you already raised them recently). Raising fees is not complicated, but it does require great Courage. I've gone through all the same worries myself. What will my clients think of me? Am I really worth more than I'm charging now? What if all of my clients leave and go to a cheaper service provider? What will my friends think of me? What will my staff think of me? Who am I to charge that much money? But it's so easy for me, why should I charge that much? Doesn't that hurt my client by charging them more?

In fact, it's the opposite. The more you charge your client, the more they value your service, and the more they take you seriously and are committed to the transformation you are offering them. Just look in your own experience. If you paid $100 for a book, and $5 for another book, and received another one for free, which one are you going to cherish more? My guess is the $100 book.

The master skill in business, the skill that solves all problems, is mastering the skill of sales. Selling is not complicated, but it can be incredibly hard when you don't have confidence in the value of your service. When you doubt yourself, your clients can feel it, and it creates doubt in them, and they are hesitant to buy. When you have unwavering confidence in yourself, and you know your value and your worth, your clients can feel that too. They feel that you are confident, not only in yourself, but also in them.

You have to be just as confident in your client as you are confident in yourself. In fact, your client is coming to you because they are scared, confused, hurting, struggling with the problem that you can solve. You need to have an energy about you that says don't worry. We've seen this problem before. We are experts in solving this problem. We can solve this problem for you, and we are going to have fun while we do it. And it's going to be easy, and you don't have to worry anymore. All you have to do is say yes, and let us take care of it for you. Without that confidence, doubt creeps in and ruins the sale.

Let's talk for a minute about why people have such a hard time selling. Selling can be uncomfortable, because we have all had experiences of making the wrong decision, or buying the wrong thing, or feeling like we wasted money. Those are all stories that we have told ourselves: that a decision was wrong. We don't want to make the same mistake again, so we become conscious with our money. I know that was my circumstance, after having several experiences where I felt that spending money was wrong, and wasting money was a horrible mistake.

And I knew how much it hurt me to spend money, so I didn't want to hurt my clients. I thought the best thing I could do for them was to offer a discount or even give my service to them for free, like a friend would. But what I learned was that I was actually robbing my clients of the highest quality experience I could provide. And I was giving myself an excuse to do less than I was capable of, because my price was so low they couldn't possibly expect a world-class experience. Now I offer premium pricing for world-class experiences, and everyone benefits. I feel honoured for my value. I honour my clients for the courage it takes to make a substantial investment and then expect me to be the best in the world, and I do not disappoint.

I've led my clients through similar experiences. Remember the story when I spent $160 on a haircut? I had to see and experience that before I could ever know what a $160 haircut would look like. I ask my clients what their service would look like if they charged 10 times what they currently charge. They don't always increase their prices by 10 times, but that exercise gives insight into what a higher value offering might look like.

For example, my friend Angela Lauria, who I hired to help me write this book, offers a five-star experience for writing a book: there's a castle, a red carpet launch, and podcast interviews. She also hires you a massage therapist, and delights and surprises every step of the way. These are all things you can only expect from a premium experience. Can you learn how to write a book for free? Absolutely. There are unlimited resources available to people who want to write a book. Could you hire a book coach for a few hundred dollars? Absolutely, but don't expect much. You get what you pay for, and when you want the best in the world you must be prepared to invest substantially.

You can be the best in the world. It takes Courage to step into that identity, but I want to share with you an important insight on being the best in the world. The world can be as small as you want it to be. Being the best in the world doesn't mean being the best on planet Earth out of 7 billion people. Being the best in the world means being the best in your community and your marketplace and your industry.

There's a bakery across the street from my house. They make the absolute best croissants in the region. People travel from 20 to 30 minutes away just to get these fresh made croissants before they sell out. They may not be the best croissants on planet Earth, but they are the best that you can buy fresh, within driving distance. And they don't make donuts. They don't make cookies. They don't make cakes. They make a few bread products, and they are the best. They've chosen their world, and they have chosen to be the best. Not the cheapest, not the most convenient, but the best.

What do you want your business to be the best at? Do you have the Courage to boldly claim that you are the best in your world? Courage sometimes means seeing your success differently. Instead of trying to be everything to everyone, choose to be the best at one specific thing, in one specific area, and dominate that space.

I worked as a business advisor for a business incubator called Invest Ottawa for about five years. In that period of time, I met with hundreds of entrepreneurs who had a similar go-to-market strategy. The strategy was this: they were going to do the same thing as everyone else, and they were going to do it cheaper. Same thing, less money.

That business model is really hard to make successful in the service business. It might work for high-volume product production, where you can streamline operations and make one million widgets, but for someone who sells their services, it's much easier to decide to become the best, to choose the world that you want to be the best in, and to commit to being the best. This takes Courage. If you're not used to self-promotion, or calling yourself the best, or being willing to own your value, deciding to be the best takes Courage.

In the beginning, you need to be confident enough to say, "I am the best solution to this problem that you can find." Once you have a few satisfied clients, they will start doing your marketing for you. You get their testimonials, and they will refer more people like them. So let me warn you, if you don't like the kinds of clients you currently have, you must have the Courage to start serving the clients that you aspire to have.

Remember Cathy, the interior designer? She was winning government contracts to do what she describes as "boring work". She said, "If I have to design one more bathroom, I may lose my mind." She had lost excitement, but it had become the bread-and-butter of her business, so she felt trapped and that she had to continue to do this boring, low margin work. I asked her, if she could do any kind of interior design work, what would it be. She knew right away. She wanted to create cool, funky, exciting office space, for high-tech companies like the Google offices or the Facebook offices: places that are famous for being fun and creative spaces that attract the best talent in the world. So we came up with a bold plan.

We identified the five CEOs of tech companies that would be dream clients for her. I asked her to write them each a love letter, and turn it into a video. She told me she hated video, she hated the sound of her voice recorded, and she said she wasn't good with technology. But we worked through the fear by realizing that if only one of those clients hired her, it would transform her business. I asked her if she was willing to be uncomfortable for a few moments in order to transform her business to do more interesting work.

So we shot five quick and simple videos with her iPhone and sent them to each CEO. I wish I could tell you it was that simple, and they hired her right away. It would make for a great story. Two of them didn't respond, and the other three all sent replies from their secretary that they weren't interested. Cathy was not at all fazed. She had already had the courage to take action, and she was prepared to take more action. She wrote handwritten letters. She asked her network if they would make introductions. And, while none of those companies have hired her company yet, she has now started getting inquiries from other technology companies who want cool, funky, creative office spaces. Now she's starting to build her portfolio of interesting creative office spaces. And maybe one day one of those five companies will hire her, or maybe they never will, but she is now doing the work that she wanted to do, and it started by having the Courage to take action.

Here's the key to taking massive action. Stop thinking, and just start doing. It is the thinking that creates worrying, that creates paralysis. Trying to get it right, trying to do it right, worrying about how it can go wrong, none of that has you taking action. The only thing that helps you take action, is taking action. And taking action creates momentum to take more action. In fact, ask yourself this question. What is the one action I am resisting? Whatever comes up for you, put this book down now, and take that action. If you are not at the appropriate location to take that action, then send someone a message telling him or her that you are going to take that action and when, exactly, you will take that action. This will create accountability. In fact, send me a text message right now, and tell me the action that you are going to take and I will hold you accountable. I want you to get into action. Stop thinking about it, and start doing it. That is the secret to Courage.

Here are a few courageous actions you can consider taking right now:

- Fire your worst client

- Let go of an underperforming team member

- Raise your fees

- Make a bold announcement of a goal that scares you

- Make a significant investment in your business

- Hire a coach to get you to your next level

Pick one, and go for it! Don't think about it, just do it.

Courage is the act of taking action despite fear, despite uncertainty. The path to greatness is paved in stepping-stones of fear. What do you fear? Do that. What are you resisting? Do that. It tends to be a very accurate compass, free to determine what the most important step for you to take is. The most important step for you to take is to take action towards your biggest fear. Would you like help getting Clarity on what the most important action to take is? Why don't you and I have a strategy session? Reserve your free strategy session at www.majeedm.com/strategy. Let's do this!

Sometimes resistance and fear can be a bit mysterious. It's like a blind spot you can't see. You don't know why, but for some reason, problems stay around no matter how hard you try. For me, I had a blind spot around money. No matter how much money I made, I always ended up being broke and in debt. I thought maybe I wasn't smart with money, so I needed to hire a financial advisor. Or I thought if I made more money it would solve my problems, so I should just work harder. That wasn't it either. But I made a substantial investment in a coach, Jayne Blumenthal—the seven-figure mindset mentor—who helped me realize that I had a childhood belief that was keeping me stuck.

Together we uncovered a childhood memory of my mother telling me that when I grew up I would become successful and rich, and when she grows old and sick I would be able to take care of her. I remember, as a kid, thinking, "I don't want you to grow old and sick," and, "I don't want to be responsible to take care of you." So somehow my mind twisted that into thinking that as long as I stay broke, my mom won't grow old and sick, and I won't be responsible for her. That was a huge insight for me. So Jayne and I did some work to release that belief, and all of a sudden it felt energetically okay to actually start saving money and getting myself out of debt.

My guess is you probably have a blind spot. And, until you identify that blind spot and release whatever belief is keeping that blind spot in place, it will be like driving with the parking brake on. You can drive with the parking brake on. And you know you could be going faster. You're not sure why you're going so slowly and have so much resistance. But instead of releasing the parking break, because you don't know the parking brake is on, you just push the gas pedal down harder and harder. What I do in my strategy calls, every single time, is identify the parking brake in your life and your business right now. And when people hire me, they are hiring me to help them release the parking break, and keep it off for good. That results in ease, and flow like they have never experienced before.

Rebecca worked at a professional services firm with a staff

of six people. She was always the first one to the office and the last one to leave. She paid herself just a little bit more than the rest of her staff, and when cash flow was tight, some months she would pay her staff but not pay herself. She loved her staff, and she loved her clients, and she always went out of her way to give them the best support. Meanwhile, she didn't have any energy left to support herself. This caused her to have occasional quiet breakdowns—crying at the office, driving home late at night asking herself how much longer she could keep up working this hard, and asking herself why this hard work hadn't amounted to much more income than she ever made back when she was at her safe, secure, traditional job.

When we started working together I asked about her childhood and what she observed to be normal at home. When it came to career and personal life balance, she told me about her dad who owned an accounting firm with a small staff, very similar to her business, and he was the first to work at the office and the last to leave. Sound familiar?

I asked Rebecca if her dad had similar values when it came to taking care of his employees and his clients. She went on to describe her father as her hero, as setting the bar in business. He was a man that all of his employees loved, and all of his clients called their friend. She told me over 1,000 people showed up to his funeral, many of them were clients, employees, and suppliers. It sounded like a legend. When I asked about how he was as a father or a husband, the tone changed. She started making excuses for him. Saying he was such a hard worker, and he did his best, and he provided for the family, and you can't be all things to all people. Sounded like a line she had practiced over and over, to tell herself why it was okay to work so hard.

"Did your father know you were such a hard worker?" I asked her. She smiled, that kind of smile that comes from the father's love for his daughter. She said, "Yes, he was proud of me."

"What would your father say if you only work 20 hours a week?" I asked her. She thought about it for a second. "I don't know. I guess he would be okay with it."

"Do you think he would be as proud of you, if you worked only part time?"

She could see where this was going. "My dad always loved me, no matter what," she said with the same tone she had when she was explaining her father's shortcomings.

We did an experiential exercise, where we invited her father's spirit into the room to have a conversation with her. I invited her to tell her father that she planned to stop working so hard, would be taking better care of herself, and spending more time with her family. I invited her to forgive her father for not being there for her when she needed him. I invited her to tell her father that she knows he will love her no matter how hard she works or how much money she makes, that he'll always be proud of her. She started to weep uncontrollably.

That was the block that needed to be released. Though he had long ago passed away, she needed to feel that her father would love her, even if she didn't work so hard and even if she started putting her own needs first.

Sometimes it takes Courage to work less. It takes Courage to put your own needs first. It takes Courage to value yourself enough to pay yourself first. It takes Courage to turn away business that you know isn't a right fit, even when you feel like you desperately need the money. It takes Courage to spend money on yourself and your business even when you're not 100 percent sure it's going to work out. It takes Courage to invest in a coach because you know you will have to face your demons and to hire a world-class team that will challenge you to conquer your fear.

The following three areas are where you can begin to take your Courage to the next level: Investing in Yourself, Public Speaking, and Sales.

Investing In Yourself

For the first five years that I was trying to grow my business on the side while having a full-time job, I never felt comfortable spending money on myself or in my business.

I remember when I was just starting my training business, I was walking through the aisles of Staples®, the office supply store, looking at all the beautiful little toys I would have "one day", once I was a successful professional speaker. I felt like I didn't have permission to buy anything that was not essential. I came across these Sharpie® markers; it was a variety pack, multi-coloured, specially designed for flip chart paper because it doesn't bleed through onto the other pages. It was a six-pack for $4.99. I held it in my hand and thought, "Do I really need this?" The answer was "no". I didn't have an immediate need for it. I convinced myself it would be a waste. Then I told myself I might be able to get it for free if I get hired to deliver training somewhere else. I left the store empty-handed. But I also felt ashamed because I didn't feel that my business was worth spending five dollars to have the right tools to be ready for the clients that I was wishing and hoping to have.

Don't get me wrong, having Sharpie® markers does not automatically give you clients. But spending money on yourself and on your business is an energetic sign of confidence in yourself and your future. It took me far too long to realize this. I would talk to consultants that I knew could help me with my marketing and with my sales, but I always resisted spending money with them. And by the way, guess who I attracted to my business? I attracted people in the same energetic space as me. They knew I could help them. They wanted me to help them. But they couldn't get themselves to spend the money. Like attracts like.

The first major investment I made in my business was to join the Canadian Association of Professional Speakers (CAPS). I sought out the most successful members and asked them about how they sold their services. That's where I met Tom Stoyan, Canada's sales coach. He taught me the script that I use today to land speaking and training gigs, and coaching clients. That one skill has accounted for many hundreds of thousands of dollars in my business. In fact, that skill was what transformed my business from moonlighting part-time to full-time.

Once I knew how to sell, it became so much easier, and it still requires Courage because every conversation in sales has the possibility to feel rejected. Over time you build resilience, but you always need to have Courage to keep taking action.

Public Speaking

Public speaking is one of the best ways I know of to market yourself and your services. Because I believe people buy you first, your idea second, and a product or service third. When you have the opportunity to speak publicly, tell your story. People want to know who you are, and some fall in love with you and your story. To those who resonate with your story, you become a category of one, and you stand out from all the other service providers you used to think of as competition.

Many people have a fear of public speaking, because it triggers the fear of rejection. What if they don't like me? What if they don't believe me? What if they think I'm a phony?

I know. I experience all the same fears, every single time I get on stage. The difference between great public speakers and people who hate public speaking, is that great public speakers know how to use the fear as energy and channel that energy into enthusiasm.

I invite you to be courageous with public speaking. Stop thinking about it, and start doing it more often. Speak up at meetings. Offer to be the guest speaker at the next networking event, host your own event, and learn how to tell your story in a way that compels people to see the world as you see the world. When you can tell your story of how you came to be in the position you are, the expert you are, they will want to help then. They will want to hire you. You are an expert in the problem that your client has. You solve that problem day in and day out. Your client may be experiencing the problem that you solve for the first time. Show them confidently that you understand the problem, and tell your story, so that they feel like you understand.

One of my clients, Melissa, hired me to help her create more sales from her live events. She is a wealth manager for high net worth individuals, and often hosted events where she would present an investment opportunity to current and prospective clients. She reached out to me and explained that she is really comfortable with the numbers, and she's comfortable talking to her clients one-on-one, but whenever she gets on stage, she freezes and feels like an idiot. I attended one of her events and watched her present. I could tell she was uncomfortable, but it really wasn't that bad. It was obvious Melissa knew what she was talking about. But by the end of the presentation, I didn't know anything more about her, other than she was good with numbers, and the investment opportunity sounded pretty legitimate. But I couldn't answer the critical question, "Why should I buy from you?"

We met after the event, and I tried to figure out her story. I asked her about her childhood and why she got into this business. She told me that her favourite toy as a child was her Snoopy calculator. Her mother made comments that she didn't dress up as a princess, or play with dolls, but she loved her little Snoopy calculator. She was the only girl on the math team and she helped her parents with their taxes when she was 12 years old. "That's gold!" I told her.

When I asked her about why wealth was important to her, she told me an emotional story about how her father lost money on the stock market, and they had to sell their house, which eventually led to her parents separating.

She had never made the connection that her line of work was a way to heal her family's drama that was caused by losing wealth. She looked me in the eye with fierce conviction and said, "I wouldn't want that to happen to anybody. That's why I fight so hard for my clients. That's why I never put the client in a position where they can lose it all."

"Melissa! You have to tell that story!" The blood drained from her face and the energy out of her body. Then she sat back in the chair, and she said, "I can't. I don't want to ruin my father's name like that."

Ah ha! You have uncovered the blind spot. It takes Courage to tell the story. There is an emotional charge, and resistance, in the story. We worked together to find a way to tell the story that honours her father and honours her mother and her family.

I know the feeling of not having the Courage to tell my story fully. There was a time when I believed my parents had failed at marriage, because I believed that divorce was the definition of a failed marriage. It wasn't until I came across a quote from Neil Strauss in his book The Truth that says, "Most people seem to believe that if a relationship doesn't last until death, it's a failure. But the only relationship that's truly a failure is one that lasts longer than it should."

That was a good change of perspective for me.

If you feel resistance to telling your story, you may need a way to tell it that honours your past and is not charged with shame. I can help you do that. Book a free strategy call with me. Email me at majeed@majeedm.com or shoot me a text message at 1-613-292-1159.

Sales

It has been said that sales solves all problems. If you have a problem in your business, chances are that growing your revenue will help you solve that problem. If you want to serve more people, serve at a deeper level, and make a bigger impact, then you must master sales.

Most people don't like to be "sales-y" and think that they need to be pushy in order to sell. Let me help you rethink selling so that you can see how the more you sell, the more you serve. Try on this new definition of Sales. "Selling is helping people make a buying decision." There are people out there that you can help, if they just make the decision to be helped by you. You can help them with that decision. It may make you and them a bit uncomfortable, because they need to get in touch with their pain in order to admit to themselves that the problem is important enough to solve. That's where you need to have courage to push through the discomfort, so that you can help them make the right decision.

The other reason why sales requires courage is that we are hardwired to fear rejection. Our caveman brain says rejection = death, so we want to avoid it. It's the same reason why public speaking is the number one fear in the world, because it puts us at risk for rejection. The key here is to know that not everyone will say "yes" to your offer, and it has nothing to do with you. In fact, it has everything to do with your offer. Change the offer, and they might say "yes". Also, remember that most sales happen after seven "no's". So when you hear a prospective client say "no", tell yourself A) they are not rejecting you—they are rejecting your offer, and B) "no" really just means "not yet".

To improve your skills in sales, practice putting yourself in uncomfortable positions and your comfort zone will expand. Courage is like a muscle that grows with practice.

Finally, you must believe in yourself and your offer (product or service). You must be 100 percent sold that your offer is totally worth it, and your customer wins when they say "yes", and you genuinely feel sorry for them when they say "no". The most important sale you ever make is the sale you make to yourself that you are worth it. This act alone will build your confidence and boost your courage.

I go into great depth into how to sell your services without selling your soul in my $1997 sales course, Selling With Heart. I'm offering it as a gift to you because I think mastering sales is the key for you to become a Fearless Leader! Claim this course and other free gifts at www.smallbiztrap.com.

Courage

- Is the act of taking action despite fear

- Means feeling less trapped

- Can change your circumstances

- Means taking massive action (stop thinking and start doing)

- Let's you step into who you want to be

- Is a muscle that grows with practice

- Grows through investing in yourself, public speaking, and sales

Claim your free gifts at www.smallbiztrap.com.

Chapter 6

The Biggest Mistakes That Will Keep You Trapped

When you decide to take your life and business to a new level, to change how you identify yourself, to step into your greatness, one thing consistently happens. All of your garbage that you think you've dealt with starts to come up. I call this the sleeping dragon. Beware of sleeping dragons. As you awaken your soul to its higher purpose, you also awaken the sleeping dragons. Prepare to slay those dragons.

My sleeping dragon was the judgment I faced from my family when I started making large sums of money. I was proud of myself, so I wanted to share with the people I love. They were not as happy for me as I had hoped they would be. Of course they congratulated me and made some comments, like, "So now you can take us all on a cruise, right?" But not long passed before those comments seemed to have a bit more judgment. "Come on, you make $20,000 in a weekend, you can afford to help me out a bit." "Wow, it must be nice to take two months vacation."

This triggered all sorts of sleeping dragons for me: the fear of being rejected from my family and no longer fitting in; the fear of having to take care of everyone else's problems; the fear of my parents growing old and sick, and having to take care of them; the fear that all that I have worked so hard for has been for nothing, because I'm just going to lose it all anyway, spending it on useless garbage.

One of my clients, Susan—a personal trainer and nutrition coach—had been visiting her parents in their retirement home twice a week, driving an hour each way, effectively giving up two nights per week with her kids and her husband.

When we started working together, I asked her to experiment with going once a week and then once every two weeks and ultimately once a month. That felt scary for her, because she felt an obligation, as a good daughter, to visit frequently. Her brothers and sisters were living far away, so the burden was on her. But that's the problem: it felt like a burden. She never looked forward to it, and she always wanted to leave as quickly as possible.

I asked her if her parents would rather see her in a good mood less frequently or in a bad mood as often as they were seeing her. It sounded logical, but these dragons don't listen to logic. We had to work on her identity as her definition of a good daughter. When she chose to live life on her own terms, it had a domino effect on different areas of her life.

She stopped spending time with friends she didn't really like. She said no to meetings with prospective clients when she had a bad gut feeling about it. She used to take those meetings and kick herself and say, "I knew they were not a fit from the first minute on the call. Why did I spend half a day driving across town to meet with them?" She had developed an internal compass for knowing what would fit her criteria as a good use of her time.

But she had to face the dragon of possibly disappointing her parents. In the end, her parents were supportive of her decision to come less frequently, because they knew it was the right thing for her to do.

Now that you know the four steps I've shared with you in this book, here's why most people don't do them.

The first step, Clarity, is always the hardest. It is unsettling to realize that you don't actually know what you want, even though you may have spent a lifetime feeling like you weren't getting what you wanted. It takes some effort to really get clear on who you are and what your business would look like if you really lived up to your full potential. It's hard, because as you gain Clarity, that also brings Clarity to your fears, and you have to face them head-on. That's why I do this work in a safe, loving space, at my retreats, or in my one-on-one coaching. It's hard to do. And if you really did the work from the Clarity chapter, then I honour you with all of my heart.

If you were successful in creating Clarity of what your life looks like at 10 out of 10 in each of the categories, and defined the gap between where you are and where you want to be, then you may have gotten stuck in the section with Commitment and making a decision. It can be hard to make a decision, because it feels like you are killing off all the other options when you choose one. It's like when I was at the food court, and I had to choose one meal, and I was afraid I was missing out on all the other flavours. Here's something that may be helpful: You must make a decision. And you must decide what you want to do first. What happens after that? Anything is possible. You can do everything, you just can't do everything first. What are you deciding to do first? Focus on that and nothing else.

The second step is Creativity. You need to ask yourself creative questions to find new ways of doing things. With Creativity, you will find ways of getting from where you are to where you want to be in a way that is easy and fun for you. People mess up this step by not taking the time to ask these expansive questions. Or, if they do ask, they don't take the time to write down as many answers as possible. Take the time to ask the questions, and you will be amazed by the insights you discover.

Step three is Commitment. You need to move out of "wanting" your goals and move into "I will ... no matter what." It's a completely different energy to be wishing for results versus being fully committed to results. You must make the decision and fully embrace it. What holds people back at this step is that they don't have true Clarity of what they really want. Or, you know what you want, but it is somehow conflicted with your values. So, go back to Creativity, and ask yourself, "How can I have exactly what I want without compromising my values."

The fourth step is Courage. Take massive action in spite of fear. The reason people get stuck at this stage is that they allow themselves to get busy and let "life get in the way." You don't need to overcomplicate and over think this step. Just start taking action, even if it's the wrong action, it's better than no action. Don't think. Just act.

You may decide to go forward on your own and not get the support you need.

Yes, you probably know you should raise your prices, and you should say more "no's" to clients that are not a fit, and you should set standards for yourself and live by them. But you knew that before you even read this book, didn't you? I know the feeling, all too well. "Hey, I'm smart. I can figure this out on my own." And yes, you are smart. And yes, you can figure this out on your own. But if you have been going it alone so far, how has it been working out for you? Look, this doesn't need to be hard. You don't need to struggle. If you still believe that business is supposed to be hard, you are buying into the hustle and grind hype. You just need to start taking lots of action. Taking action means you have to let go of your excuses, and decide that now is your time to shine.

No world-class athlete or world-class performer of any kind would ever dare consider going it alone. Part of me wishes I would've hired a coach sooner, and part of me knows that I wasn't ready to hire a coach before I did. Are you ready to get the support that will make your journey easier, less painful, and help you make the impact and the income that you know you have the potential to make? I would love to be your coach, and if you would like to book a free strategy session with me, I will help you create a plan to achieve your goals and we will see if you are ready for coaching. Book a free strategy session with me at www.majeedm.com/strategy.

Claim your free gifts at www.smallbiztrap.com.

Chapter 7

Next Steps for
the Fearless Leader

I hope this book gives you Clarity, Creativity, Commitment, and Courage. I hope you read this book again and again, because I think you will find parts that didn't land for you the first time that may land for you the second or third time. You can revisit this book at different points in your life, and get different things. My biggest wish for you is that you make the decision that now is your time to shine and that you choose to become a Fearless Leader. I hope that you choose to forever leave the cult of mediocrity, and only surround yourself with the best people in the world. I hope you upgrade your friends by choosing to be with the people that excite you and challenge you.

Before we part ways, I want you to take a moment to pull out your calendar. Pick a date and time, the sooner the better, that you commit to taking your first step to becoming a Fearless Leader. I'm guessing that first step will be some form of sending a communication. It may be a text message, email, phone call, or a post on social media. It will be a declaration of a commitment. I will wait no matter what. I will lose 20 pounds in the next two months no matter what. I will quit smoking today. I will make 10 sales calls tomorrow. I will make an offer to five people this week, and these are the five people. Write it down. If you're not clear on exactly what your next step should be, I invite you to call me, and I will help you find your best next step.

As the highest rated trainer in the world for one of the largest training companies in the world, Learning Tree International, I've trained over 1000 professionals. Over and over I met incredibly talented people who didn't see their own gifts. In conversations I would have between training sessions, I would help them see the higher version of themselves that somehow I could clearly see, but they could not.

Time and again, they told me that was the conversation that they needed to have, more important than all the training on psychology, communication, and leadership skills. I believe it was the act of having someone care enough for them to believe in them, and to see them in their highest potential, so that they could see it themselves. That is the transformational moment that is so fulfilling about the work that I do. I believe my gift is to see the talent in my client and show them so they can see it and believe in themselves too.

The results? My clients' self-worth goes up. They value themselves more, and so they can more easily sell themselves to their clients. Sales go up. Cash flow goes up. They reinvest in themselves and their business, and they have the confidence and feel the security to finally start putting their own needs first. They take care of themselves, which allows them to be more present and focused, to show up in a bigger way, which ultimately transforms the culture of their office.

In a small business, the founder sets the tone of the culture. Upgrade the founder, and you upgrade the culture of the company. It's incredible to witness.

I've seen entire offices lose weight and become healthier, once the founder started taking care of her health.

I've seen margins go up and sales increase, when the client started turning low-margin business away and going after bigger and better clients with more and more confidence.

You are a business owner. You are an entrepreneur. You are a living brand. Now it's your time to be a Fearless Leader.

Claim your free gifts at www.smallbiztrap.com.

Acknowledgements

To my clients who continue to humble me by their heroic acts of love. To my wife for her undying support, for fiercely loving our children, and for being my best friend. To Angela Lauria for being an inspirational Fearless Leader, calling me on my bullsh*t, and refusing to let me continue to play small.

To the Morgan James Publishing team: Special thanks to David Hancock, CEO & Founder for believing in me and my message. To my Managing Editor, {insert name}, thanks for making the process seamless and easy. Many more thanks to everyone else, but especially Jim Howard, Bethany Marshall, and Nickcole Watkins.

About the Author

Majeed Mogharreban is on a mission to help entrepreneurs and change-makers create a life of purpose and service through business. Majeed started his first business when he was 16 years old. By the age of 21 he had travelled to 24 countries and started five businesses. Majeed has coached professional athletes, members of parliament, a two-time gold medal winning Olympian, and an executive of a Fortune 500 company. With a focus to serve small businesses making a big impact in the community, Majeed teaches proven strategies to increase profits and have more fun in business. Majeed lives with his incredible wife Elaine, daughter Ruby, and son Charles in Gatineau, Quebec, Canada.

Website: www.majeedm.com

Email: majeed@majeedm.com

Facebook: https://www.facebook.com/majeed.mogharreban

Twitter: https://twitter.com/MajeedM

Thank You

Dear Fearless Leader,

Thank you for reading *The Small Business Trap*. I am honoured and humbled that you would give me your most precious resource, your attention. My hope is that your time has been well spent. Now it's time to put it all into action.

Go to www.smallbiztrap.com to claim your free gifts, including...

- Access to my $1997 sales course, Selling With Heart, to learn how to "sell your services without selling your soul." Growing your sales will dramatically speed up your ability to create the life and business you want.

- Special Report: Grant-Getting Secrets To Win Free Government Money ($97 value).

- Free one-on-one Freedom Formula Strategy Session ($997 value). Book your free strategy session with me at www.majeedm.com/strategy.

I am honoured that you have taken the time to pick up this book, and you can consider me your friend. Please reach out by email at majeed@majeedm.com or phone or text at 1-613-292-1159.

Here's to your success!
Majeed